DAILY LIFE

The American Frontier

Melanie Ann Apel

KIDHAVEN
PRESS™

THOMSON

GALE

San Diego • Detroit • New York • San Francisco • Cleveland
New Haven, Conn. • Waterville, Maine • London • Munich

© 2003 by KidHaven Press. KidHaven Press is an imprint of The Gale Group, Inc., a division of Thomson Learning, Inc.

KidHaven™ and Thomson Learning™ are trademarks used herein under license.

For more information, contact
KidHaven Press
27500 Drake Rd.
Farmington Hills, MI 48331-3535
Or you can visit our Internet site at http://www.gale.com

LIBRARY OF CONGRESS CATALOGING-IN-PUBLICATION DATA

Apel, Melanie Ann.
   The American Frontier / by Melanie Ann Apel.
    v. cm. — (Daily life)
Summary: Discusses daily life on the American frontier, reasons and methods of moving families westward, establishing homes and farms, day to day life on the frontier, and building of communities and towns.
Includes bibliographical references and index.
   ISBN 0-7377-1528-6 (alk. paper)
   1. Frontier and pioneer life — West (U.S.) — Juvenile literature. 2. Pioneers — West (U.S.) — History — 19th century — Juvenile literature. 3. Pioneers — West (U.S.) — Social life and customs — 19th century — Juvenile literature. 4. West (U.S.) — History — 1860–1890 — Juvenile literature. [1. Frontier and pioneer life. 2. Pioneers — West (U.S.) 3. West (U.S.) — History — 1860–1890.] I. Title. II. Series.
   F596 .A59 2003
   978' .02—dc21
                             2002013942

Printed in the United States of America

Contents

CHAPTER ONE

Moving On, Moving In

I n the 1800s, people traveled from the east to the west across the United States in search of land and opportunity. The Homestead Act of 1862, which was signed by President Abraham Lincoln, allowed any American citizen who was at least twenty-one years old to file a claim for free land that belonged to the government.

The Homestead Act was passed to encourage people to settle the vast empty prairies in the public domain west of the Mississippi River. If people improved on the land they occupied, such as farming or building a home there, in five years the land became their own property.

When people heard about the rich soil and the good hunting out west, as well as the free land, they became very excited. As one would-be settler told his wife, "The hunting's good in the west. A man can get all the meat he wants."[1] Some families decided to move to find land that had richer soil, which would give them better crops. Some moved because they heard there was better weather in other parts of the country. Others were out of work and wanted to try their hand at farming.

Most people who came to settle the new land were families, but occasionally a single man or a widow and her children set out to make the trip as well. Once they decided to go west, everything in the house had to be either packed up or left behind. Most people brought along as many of their belongings as they could fit inside their covered wagon.

President Abraham Lincoln signed the Homestead Act which encouraged people to move west.

Preparing to Travel

The family's clothes, the pots and pans and dishes, the bedding, the furniture, the family Bible, and any other belongings were snugly arranged inside the wagon. Food such as biscuits, bread, vegetables, and fruits were packed as well. People realized, however, that when their food supplies ran out, they would have to rely on the land.

Families traveled west in covered wagons like this one. Belongings that did not fit in the wagon had to be left behind.

The family made the covered wagon ready for travel. First, they had to rub oil over a large canvas to make it waterproof. Then they stretched the canvas across large wooden hoops that reached from one side of the wagon to the other. Strings on the ends of the canvas allowed the wagon to be closed up. This kept rain and wind outside, while the family stayed warm and dry inside.

When the wagon was ready to go and all the belongings had been packed, the family's horses or mules were harnessed to the front of the wagon. A wooden board attached to the front of the wagon served as the driver's and passengers' seats. The driver (usually the father) held the reins and, with the horses pulling, drove the wagon along the dusty road. Children usually stayed inside the wagon during the journey.

Making the Journey

The road across country was long and lonely. Travelers covered only about twelve to twenty miles per day. In 1864, a woman named Pamelia Fergus wrote about her family's trip in a covered wagon. "I can tell you nothing only that we're here and it's strange," she said. "I wish we had never started. . . . It seems impossible to get there."[2]

Sometimes the adults would walk alongside the wagons to give the horses a break. There was not much to see as they walked along—just miles and miles of empty prairie and the beautiful sky above. "As far as they could see, to the east and to the south and to the west, nothing was moving on all the vastness of the High Prairie. Only green grass was rippling in the wind, and white clouds drifted in the high, clear sky,"[3] said Laura Ingalls Wilder, recalling one of the numerous trips across the prairie that she and her family made.

Traveling across the barren plains was an adventure, but it was also very difficult. Most people began their journey in New England. They traveled hundreds of miles to arrive at land that would later become the states of Wisconsin, Indiana, Ohio, Missouri, and Illinois. Many even went as far west as California. In addition to traveling by covered wagon, people also traveled on horses, on mules, or by foot. Unlike today when a person can fly across the country in a matter of hours or even drive from coast to coast in just a few days, a trip by covered wagon took months.

Often, a family would not see any other people for days or even weeks while traveling. There was nothing at all but empty land. One settler described the journey this way:

A man must be able to endure heat like a salamander . . . dust like a toad. . . . He must learn to eat with his unwashed fingers, drink out of the same vessel as his mules, sleep on the ground when it rains, and share his blanket with **vermin,** and have patience with mosquitoes.[4]

Wagon Trains

While some families found themselves alone on the prairie, others met up and traveled together in a wagon train. In a wagon train, wagons traveled in a single-file line with enough space between them to avoid getting covered in each other's dust. The wagon train stopped at mealtime and at night. The drivers drew their wagons into a circle. Everyone felt safe and protected inside the circle of wagons.

A wagon train provided more than safety in numbers. If a family ran out of food or dry clothing or if their wagon needed a repair, they could count on the other families to help out. When the families in the

Some families traveled west alone. It was possible to travel for weeks without seeing other people.

wagon train stopped each day, the men hunted and the women cooked meals. The children stretched their legs and played with each other. When it got dark, just before everyone went to sleep, the families gathered around a campfire and sing songs or tell stories.

Even when families were part of a wagon train, traveling across country was still challenging. Water crossings, such as at the Missouri River or the Colorado River, were especially difficult. If the water was fairly shallow, the driver of the wagon urged the horses to pull the

Overland Routes to the West

Many families traveled west together in wagon trains, so they could help each other during the trip.

wagon across the river. If the water was deep, the animals had to swim across.

Some people had made their wagons waterproof by sealing up the cracks between the boards. They attempted to float the wagon across the river. Often, when many wagons traveled across the same river, a flatboat called a

Travelers used flatboats like this one to take their wagons safely across rivers.

scow was built to take the wagons safely to the other side of the river. No matter what method was used, these river crossings were often unpredictably dangerous, and families could lose animals, people, or supplies before they reached the other side.

Bad weather also made the trip difficult. Storms brought strong winds, harsh rains, and deep mud, making it hard for the horses and mules to keep their footing and stay on the trail. Sometimes the trip was slowed down even more by the heat. When it was very hot, the animals had to rest more often.

Despite the hardships of travel, most families did not turn back. They continued their journey with the hopes and dreams of the better life that lay ahead.

CHAPTER TWO

Settling into a New Way of Life

After months of weary travel, settlers reached the new land they would call home. The land was wilderness with nothing around but some trees, a lot of grass, rocks, and a stream or river for water. Laura Ingalls Wilder remembers settling on such land. "I could see a creek . . . a grassy bank, and beyond it a line of willow tree tops. . . . Everywhere else the prairie grasses were rippling far away to the sky's straight edge,"[5] she said.

When the settlers first arrived at their destination, they had to start from scratch to build a new life. Each family had to establish its own homestead. Most of the settlers chose land on which there were trees. Every member of the family pitched in to help. Men and women and even the older children set to work chopping down trees. After the logs were trimmed, they were used to make the walls of a log cabin.

Building Houses

Most log cabins had one large room. Sometimes a part of the room was sectioned off to give the parents a bit of privacy while they slept. The children might sleep in a loft built above the room, or they snuggled up on the floor or in one bed all together.

Spaces were left for windows in log cabins, but no glass was available. Instead, paper soaked in oil covered the window openings. This allowed light to filter through. A strong door with a latch was necessary to keep wild animals and strong winds out of the cabin.

Laura Ingalls Wilder wrote about her family's trip west and the life they lived there.

Log cabins did not have electricity or indoor plumbing. People woke up at sunrise and went to bed at sunset. Candles or kerosene lamps were used in darkness. There were no bathrooms in log cabins, either. Instead, an **outhouse,** a small wooden structure, was used outside the

Settlers chop down trees and used the logs to build cabins.

Most log cabins had just one room, and they did not have running water or electricity.

house, usually located off to the side of the cabin or back a few yards. Inside the outhouse was a plank of wood with a hole in it. The wood was set over the top of a wooden box. A large hole was dug below the box.

In addition to the log cabin and outhouse, most families built one more structure on their land. Not far from the log cabin was a barn to house the family's animals. The settlers relied on animals for food and for farming.

A farmer plows his field. Frontier families had to plant their own crops.

Farming

The American frontier family had to be self-sufficient. Their food had to be found, caught, or grown. "A farmer depends on himself, and the land and the weather," said James Wilder, a farmer in the early 1800s. "If you're a farmer, you raise what you eat, you raise what you wear."[6]

Animals such as cows and chickens were kept for food. Most families had horses or oxen to do heavy work such as hauling or plowing. People who settled in some areas raised animals and sold them to make money. Cattle were raised for beef in Nebraska, South Dakota, and

Montana. In Wisconsin and Minnesota, settlers raised dairy cattle.

Depending on what part of the country a family settled in, different kinds of crops, including vegetables, corn, and grains, were planted. For example, in Illinois and Iowa, corn became the favored crop. In Nebraska, South Dakota, and Montana, wheat grew well. Every vegetable garden had standard vegetables such as squash, potatoes, turnips, and spinach for the family to eat.

Farming was a job that the whole family took part in every day. If a family arrived at their new home in the fall, it was very important to plant the crops right away so that in the spring and following fall food could be harvested. There was no time to waste. A bad storm, a dry season with too little rain, or a plague could wipe out a farm and leave the family with nothing to show for their hard work.

Surviving Bad Weather

In addition to the hard work that families had to do every day just to survive, they had to contend with elements that were beyond their control, such as the weather. Depending on the part of the country in which they settled, some people, even those who lived in Illinois, experienced summers that were blistering hot. Likewise, the winter in certain parts of the country, such as Wisconsin, could be very cold, with many snowstorms.

Sometimes it would get so bitterly cold that daily chores such as milking cows or fetching water were all but impossible. Snowstorms could cause snowdrifts that blocked doors, locking a family inside their house for days. Animals in the barn would be miserable as well, unfed and unmilked.

In summer, windy, dry weather could cause brushfires. Fires would start on their own simply because there had been no rain for weeks, the earth was dry as a bone,

A farmer braves the cold of a winter snowstorm to bring hay to his animals.

and the sun was so hot. "My daughter and I saw it happen ourselves," says a woman named Denise Pagel, who traveled with her daughter to California. "We were stopped on the road for a rest and we watched as a patch of scrub on the side of the hill just started smoldering and then burst into flames as we sat there!"[7] Lightning strikes could also start a brushfire.

A brushfire could destroy everything around it, leaving a family homeless and without belongings. To try to put it out, the family members had to move fast to bring water from the stream up to the fire. The first thing a family would try to save was their crops. Without crops, a family would have no food and nothing to sell to make money. It was often difficult to save the house and the barn from the flames, but everyone worked as hard as they could to save all that was precious to them. Many times, all that they could do was pray for rain as they ran back and forth hauling water to the fire.

Illness

The settlers often had more to battle than the problems caused by the weather. Illness was not uncommon among the settlers, and few doctors could be found to treat the sick. Without proper medicines, many people died from illnesses that today are considered minor, such as the flu. Some medicines, such as antibiotics and vaccines, had not been invented yet. Illnesses such as scarlet fever might leave a person blind or damage his or her heart. Parasites were common as well.

An illness called ague (which is pronounced A-gyoo) affected many settlers on the frontier. Although rarely

This family is lucky to receive the services of a doctor. Few doctors were available on the frontier.

fatal, ague—recognized today as malaria—caused high fever, chills, and shakiness. Anson Van Buren, an early 1800s settler, described getting the ague as a feeling that "crept over your system in streaks, faster and faster, and then colder and colder in successive **undulations** that coursed down your back."[8]

In frontier families, at least one child, and sometimes several children, might not make it to adulthood. Illness and the accepted death of children were among the reasons why families usually had a large number of children.

The settlers on the American frontier faced many hardships. They needed to work hard for their survival.

CHAPTER THREE

A Day at Home

Keeping the house clean, cooking, tending to the animals, making and mending clothes, keeping the house and tools in good repair, and caring for the children took a lot of time and a lot of people. Many tasks kept frontier people busy from sunup to sundown. Everyone in the family had chores to do. Even the littlest children in the family were given small tasks.

One of the chores that children often helped their mothers with was candle making. People relied on candles for light. Making candles was not hard, but it took a lot of time. To make candles, long bits of string, which would serve as wicks, were dipped in hot tallow, or animal fat, over and over again. After each dip, the tallow would have to dry and harden. When the candles were thick enough to burn for a number of hours, they were considered ready for use.

What People Ate

Perhaps the most important task to be done each day was that of preparing the food to keep the family strong and healthy for all the chores they had to do.

Families got their food from the land. Different foods were available depending on the time of year. Often, the families had to eat the same vegetables or fruits every day when they were in season.

The frontier had many natural resources. Berries grown in the wild could be gathered for mealtimes. The nearby stream was a good source of fish. Animals on the farm, called **livestock,** provided food, too, such as fresh eggs and milk. The women in the family were responsible for preparing the food.

A frontier family poses in front of their home. Chores kept every member of the family busy all day.

Cooking

The women spent a great deal of time every day preparing the family's meals. Cooking was slow because everything had to be made from scratch. The women cooked the family's meals over a wood stove or in the fireplace. They cooked things such as biscuits and cornmeal, meat, potatoes, fresh fish, onions, bacon, and sometimes desserts such as cookies or pie. Women also made dairy products such as cream, buttermilk, and butter themselves. The women tried hard to be creative so that

Women spent most of their time cooking because everything had to be made from scratch.

Men spent much of their time hunting so their families would have meat for dinner.

the family would not become bored with the food they were eating. It was unusual for women to have actual recipes to follow. They cooked using their memory as a guide.

While the women cooked, the men spent much of their time hunting for deer and rabbit. Early in the morning, the men left home on foot or on horseback, armed with a shotgun, and spent the day looking for **game.** If the hunter had a good day, the family ate meat for dinner, or maybe even for several days. If he had a bad day, there were only vegetables, fruits, or grains for dinner.

Food spoiled quickly on the frontier because it could not be kept cold. If a family had extra meat, it was dried. Dried meat can still be found today in the form of beef jerky. To dry the meat, the first step was to cut it into strips. The strips were then cooked on a low fire for a few hours or left outside for the sun to do the work. The meat was left until it was dry enough and could be saved. Catharine Beecher wrote about another method of preserving meat in *Homekeeper and Healthkeeper's Companion:*

> To preserve one hundred pounds of beef, you will need four quarts of rock salt, pounded fine; four ounces of saltpeter, pounded fine; and four pounds of brown sugar. Mix these well. Put a layer of meat in the bottom of a barrel, with a thin layer of the mixture under it. Pack the meat into the barrel in layers, and between each layer put proportions of the mixture, allowing a little more to the top layer. Then, pour in brine till the barrel is full. . . . If the brine ever looks bloody, or smells badly, it must be scalded, and more salt put to it, and poured over the meat.[9]

Fruits and vegetables that needed to be preserved were canned. Women spent hours preparing these fruits and vegetables by boiling them and adding sugar until they were ready to be put in tightly sealed jars. "A thrifty and generous provider will see to it that her store-closet is furnished with such a variety of articles that successive changes can be made in diet for a good length of time,"[10] wrote Catharine Beecher in 1873. People still can fruits and vegetables today. By preparing foods ahead of time in this manner, food was not wasted.

Keeping Everything and Everyone Clean

Taking care of the house was also hard work. Early frontier homes had dirt floors, which were impossible to keep clean. When the family had time, a wooden floor was laid and keeping clean underfoot became much easier.

Dishes were washed down at the stream or by using water brought up to the house, either from the stream or from a pump outside the house. Clothes were washed in much the same manner as washing dishes. Since people had few clothes, washing was usually done once a week.

Sometimes people bathed in a stream. They used soap that they made themselves.

Women washed clothes by hand. First they boiled the water and then they rubbed the clothes along a washboard to get them really clean. They used soap they had made themselves from a combination of a strong chemical called lye and fat from animals. The lye and animal fat were boiled together and then poured into a mold to harden. This soap was used to clean everything, including the people. After rinsing the clothes in cool water, they would be hung on a line to dry in the fresh air.

Every Sunday evening, the entire family took a bath. Sometimes people bathed in the stream. Often, however, each family member took his or her turn in the washtub, a large metal tub a person sits in to wash up. Water was brought in and warmed over the fire. The water was not changed for each family member's turn in the washtub. Imagine how dirty that water might have been by the time the youngest in the family got their turn to be scrubbed.

What People Wore

Most people on the frontier had two outfits: one to wear every day and a special outfit for church on Sunday. In the early 1800s, before towns and the first general stores, women were responsible not only for making all of the clothes for the family but also for making the fabric from which the clothes were made. Women also knitted sweaters, scarves, socks, and caps. Because making clothing was so time-consuming, everyone wore their clothes until they were completely worn out. Children passed their outgrown clothes down to their younger brothers

The cast of the *Little House on the Prairie* television series wears clothing typical of the frontier.

and sisters. The women and children also worked hard to keep all of the clothing in good repair, darning holey socks and mending torn shirts.

Women and girls wore long dresses or long skirts with long-sleeved blouses. Girls' dresses were usually bright and made of colorful cotton with patterns called gingham and calico, with flowers or checks. Under the skirt would be a petticoat and bloomers, stockings, and strong, sturdy black or brown shoes that laced up the ankle. Over their dresses, women and girls wore aprons to keep as clean as possible while cooking and doing chores. Outside in the sun, they wore bonnets, which tied in a bow under their chins. The brim of the bonnet kept the sun off their faces. It is hard to imagine doing chores and working so hard in the hot summer, wearing such a great amount of clothing.

Men and boys on the frontier wore dark pants and light shirts. Suspenders kept their pants from falling down. Men's shoes were not much different from those worn by the women, except the women's shoes some-times had a higher heel. Men also wore wide-brimmed hats to keep the sun off their faces.

The food people ate, the clothes they wore, and the things they needed for everyday life, such as soap and candles, all took time to prepare or create. This made up the day's work for families living on the American fron-tier. Each family member was expected to work hard as a matter of survival for the entire family.

CHAPTER FOUR

Making a Life

Although at first the settlers were out in the wilderness alone with no neighbors in sight, as the years went by, more homesteads began to fill the area. Neighbors moved in, built houses, and set up their own farms nearby. Still, a neighbor's house was not simply "next door" as it is today. Homes were usually at least one mile, and sometimes several miles, apart. Eventually, homesteaded areas became small towns. A doctor would move in and open a small office in or adjacent to his house. Other important buildings eventually made their way to the frontier as well.

The General Store

By the late 1800s, almost every town became large enough to have a mercantile, or general store. The general store was like a small version of today's department store or discount store. Women could buy fabric for making new dresses and shirts there. Men could buy a new hat or tools to work the farm. Children could buy books or toys or even a small piece of penny candy.

If the family was short on money, they might trade eggs for other food or supplies they needed at the general store. As an Ohio woman named Frances Trollope described, she could get things such as coffee and tea "by

Most frontier towns had a general store. Families could buy or trade for goods they needed.

sending a batch of butter and chicken"[11] to the general store.

The general store was also a place to visit with neighbors for a few minutes before returning home to chores. Men often sat together and played checkers or talked about the latest news. Children often gathered at the general store after school. They might buy a small piece of candy or just talk to each other for a while before heading out for their long walk back home.

The One-Room Schoolhouse

Most people on the prairie believed that it was important to learn to read and write, and the adults who knew how taught their children at home. Parents often used their Bible to help their children learn to read. By the late 1800s, most areas had enough families with children to start a small school and hire a teacher.

Frontier children of all ages attended school together in one-room schoolhouses.

Children went to school in one-room schoolhouses. Children of all ages were in the same classroom. The youngest, smallest children sat in the front of the class and the older children sat by grade, from youngest to oldest, all the way to the back of the classroom. A single teacher had the task of teaching all of the children, even though they were on different levels.

The teacher stood at the front of the classroom, often on a raised platform, and wrote on a large blackboard. Children practiced penmanship and math and wrote their lessons on small blackboards. Schools had very few books in the beginning, but children eventually had a **primer** and perhaps a history book. Children often had to share their books, even if they were not at the same level.

Children went to school only if their family could spare them for a few hours every day. Some children had to stay home and help on the farm.

To Church on Sunday

The schoolhouse was also used as a meeting place for events such as town meetings, suppers and church services..

Religion was an important part of everyday life on the frontier. Everyone went to church on Sunday. Not only was this a time for worship, listening to sermons, and giving thanks for land and food, Sunday was also a day of relaxation and fun. In the summer, there were often large picnic lunches after church. People looked forward to Sundays because that was the day to visit with neighbors.

Dressed in their finest clothes, settlers enjoy a picnic after church.

Worship was not limited to church on Sunday, however. Every home had its own copy of the Bible. Not only was the Bible read and studied, but it served as a record of the family's history. Many important dates, such as births, marriages, and deaths in the family, were recorded in the family Bible. The family Bible would be passed along from one generation to the next. Many people read the Bible every day.

People read other materials as well. Letters they had received were often saved to be read and reread. Others read books, newspapers, and catalogs from the general store, which showed all sorts of interesting things that could be purchased.

Time to Play

People on the frontier enjoyed what little free time they had. Children were busy with school and chores, but they also found time to play. Children played games such as **stickball,** which was a popular game similar to baseball that used a stick rather than a bat. Children also played with rag dolls and marbles.

The adults found time to relax, as well. Men would sometimes play music on instruments such as the violin or harmonica. They would also sing songs or tell elaborate stories.

Women often got together for sewing **bees** or quilting bees. During these bees, women worked on a large task, such as making a quilt, together. Sharing their tasks with

After finishing school and chores, children played games such as marbles.

A Pony Express rider leaves a post office with mail to deliver. Frontier families wrote many letters.

other women made chores such as canning, soap making, candle making, and knitting more fun. They laughed and talked and shared stories. The work went much faster than if one woman had to do it alone.

There were other get-togethers that everyone attended. Anna Fowler Nelson described her favorite gatherings in 1883: "[We enjoyed] dances . . . socials, and the occasional Christmas party. Each was an event, and all were enthusiastically attended by everyone, young and old, within reasonable distance."[12]

Many women wrote letters to their family and friends they had left behind in different parts of the country. "Keeping the family together has been the special charge of women,"[13] historian Lillian Schlissel wrote about the frontier. The first official post offices and mail routes were not set up until the mid-1860s. Before this, people gave their letters to travelers, who would drop them off in towns near the people who were to receive them. Railroad post offices and official mail service made this process a lot more precise, but it still took quite a long time for a letter to get from its writer to its reader.

Life on the American frontier was very different from life today. Family members worked hard and relied on each other for their daily needs. By working well together, people were able to turn the vast, empty prairie into homes and farms for themselves, and later into small towns that grew to become some of today's biggest cities.

Notes

Chapter One: Moving On, Moving In

1. Quoted in John E. Miller, *Where History and Literature Meet: Laura Ingalls Wilder's Little Town.* Lawrence: University Press of Kansas, 1994, p. 264.
2. Quoted in William Anderson, *The Little House Guidebook.* New York: HarperCollins, 1996, p. 21.
3. Quoted in PBS, "Homestead History," *Frontier House.* www.pbs.org.
4. Quoted in PBS, "Homestead History."

Chapter Two: Settling into a New Way of Life

5. Quoted in Anderson, *The Little House Guidebook,* p. 29.
6. Quoted in Ann Romines, *Constructing the Little House: Gender, Culture, and Laura Ingalls Wilder.* Amherst: University of Massachusetts Press, 1997, p. 37.
7. Interview with Denise Pagel, 2002.
8. Quoted in Larry B. Massie, "Voyages into Michigan's Past." http://ncha.ncats.net

Chapter Three: A Day at Home

9. Quoted in PBS, "Homestead History."
10. Quoted in PBS, "Homestead History."

Chapter Four: Making a Life

11. Quoted in Frances Trollope, "Married Life on a Forest Farm: Provisions, Entertainments," 1828. http://xroads.virginia.edu.
12. Quoted in PBS, "Homestead History."
13. Quoted in Romines, *Constructing the Little House,* p. 14.

Glossary

bee: A gathering of people to do something together, such as quilting.

game: Animals hunted for food or sport.

livestock: Animals kept or raised on a farm for use or profit.

outhouse: A small wooden shelter used as a toilet.

primer: A small book teaching children to read or teaching an introduction to a subject.

stickball: A game similar to baseball.

undulation: A wave or ripple.

vermin: Small, common harmful or objectionable animals, such as fleas or mice, that are hard to get rid of.

For Further Exploration

William Anderson, *Laura Ingalls Wilder: A Biography.* New York: HarperTrophy, 1992. This book, complete with original photos, is a concise biography of Laura Ingalls Wilder, the author who shared her life in the *Little House on the Prairie* series.

———, *The Little House Guidebook.* New York: Harper-Collins, 1996. This is a guide for travelers interested in visiting all of the places where Laura Ingalls Wilder and her family once lived. Complete with photos and maps, this guide tells how to get to each place and what else to visit while you are there.

Kristiana Gregory, *Dear America: Across the Wide and Lonesome Prairie: The Oregon Trail Diary of Hattie Campbell, 1847.* New York: Scholastic, 1997. This fictional diary of a thirteen-year-old girl takes the reader across the Oregon Trail in 1847.

Bobbie Kalman, *Life in the Old West: Women of the West.* New York: Crabtree, 2000. A beautifully illustrated book about the life of women on the prairie, the hardships they endured, and the strengths they shared. This book includes actual photographs from the 1800s.

Ellen Levine, *If You Traveled West in a Covered Wagon.* New York: Scholastic, 1986. Each illustrated page asks and answers a new question about traveling cross-country in a covered wagon in the 1800s.

John E. Miller, *Where History and Literature Meet: Laura Ingalls Wilder's Little Town.* Lawrence: University Press of Kansas, 1994. Miller explains how Laura Ingalls Wilder's *Little House* books help readers understand history. He also describes Rose Wilder Lane's efforts to publish and promote her mother's books.

Ann Romines, *Constructing the Little House: Gender, Culture, and Laura Ingalls Wilder.* Amherst: University of Massachusetts Press, 1997. This book takes a look at the life of Laura Ingalls Wilder and her relationship with her mother from a feminist point of view.

Glenn Rounds, *Sod Houses on the Great Plains.* New York: Holiday House, 1995. This is an illustrated description of people building their new homes on the prairie.

Laura Ingalls Wilder, *The Little House Books.* 9 vols. New York: HarperCollins Juvenile Books, 1999. The original nine books in the series illustrate the life of the Ingalls family in the 1800s as they traveled and made their home in various parts of the Midwest. Other books, workbooks, calendars, cookbooks, picture books, and books about the Ingalls family written by other authors are available as well.

Index

Picture Credits

About the Author

Melanie Ann Apel holds a bachelor's degree in theater arts from Bradley University and a bachelor's degree in respiratory care from National-Louis University. She has written more than 30 nonfiction books for children and young adults, and this is her second book for KidHaven Press. When she is not writing, Apel loves to read, figure skate, and spend time with friends and family, especially her beautiful baby boy. She and her husband and son live in Chicago. You may reach Apel at kidlet31@yahoo.com.